# CORRECTING YOUR CHILD IN LOVE

### A Christian Parent's Manual
### A Biblical Guide For Loving Discipline

## Abner C. Sumrall

PRESS

This manual was written in recognition of the need for clarification and simplification of Biblical principles concerning correcting our children in love as set forth in God's Holy Word, the Bible. Every effort has been made to publish an accurate, timely, and authoritative guide for loving discipline. Nothing is to be construed from this material supporting abuse of any kind. The author, reviewers, and publisher do not assume any legal responsibility for the accuracy of the text or any other contents.

This information is made available for educational use only and is not intended to be a substitute for consultation with a competent professional concerning the issues presented.

www.xulonpress.com

Here's what others are saying about CORRECTING YOUR CHILD IN LOVE:

"In his book, *Correcting Your Child In Love*, Pastor Abner Sumrall has hit a home run! In our 'politically correct' day and time, Sumrall has taken on this divisive topic and answered it with grace and truth! The reader will find this book to be warm, humorous and most all informative. I can recommend *Correcting Your Child In Love* to all parents who desire to know God's best way for their families."

> Daniel A. Tomlinson, M.D.
> Author: *Birth Pangs: How Pregnancy Reveals God's Plan for the Ages*

"Pastor Abner Sumrall's book, *Correcting Your Child In Love*, is a loving and truthful account of God's Word on the subject of child discipline. One main thought that came to my mind after reading this refreshing book is that I regret I wasn't aware of these Godly principles when I raised my own children."

Barry N. Shaw
Attorney At Law (Retired)
Writer, Father, & Grandfather

"So much of today's parenting techniques are weighted upon behavioral modification through compromise with the child, rather than pure spiritual transformation through compliance with God. In his book, *Correcting Your Child In Love*, Abner has penned the 'sweet spot' of Biblical application and provokes parents to go deeper with God in their assertive discipline of their child."

Richard Abblitt
Pastor/Director
The Mission at Carmen Serdan

# CONTENTS

# ACKNOWLEDGMENTS

First and foremost I have a heart of gratitude to our Heavenly Father. Without Him I am nothing but in Him I can do all things through Christ who strengthens me (Philippians 4:13). I am so thankful that He did not leave me to myself to figure out how to raise my children.

A special thanks to Pastor Jon Courson of Applegate Christian Fellowship for faithfully teaching the truth of the Word of God to me and my family for well over twenty five years.

Dr. James Dobson and Focus On The Family radio ministry has been a continual support for encouragement and defending family values.

The booklet, *Under Loving Command*, written by Al and Pat Fabrizio, was a significant resource for reviewing and being reminded of the importance of consistent, loving discipline, during the formative years of our children.

A note of thanks to P.K. Hallinan—renowned children's author, pastor, friend, and co-laborer in Christ—for his continual encouragement in motivating me to become a published author.

Also, I extend my gratitude to Barry Shaw, Dan Tomlinson, Rich Abblitt, Liz Lorenz, Amie Blore, and Jon-Micah Sumrall for reading through the original manuscript and offering their input and encouragement.

I express sincere appreciation to my children for teaching me the reality of lovingly and responsibly applying God's Word to our lives on a daily basis.

I am deeply indebted to my wife, Sarah; without her, none of this would have been possible. She partnered with me to love, nurture, and train our children in the ways of the Lord. In addition, I am thankful for her invaluable efforts in proofing and editing the multiple revisions of the original manuscript in order to bring this book into being.

# FOREWORD

During our thirty years of marriage I have been blessed and thankful for Ab's passion for the Word of God and his desire to be obedient to the commandments therein. I was encouraged and impressed by the manner in which he disciplined our children: lovingly, patiently, and in direct obedience to the Bible. I had never witnessed discipline in such a loving, consistent manner. He simply obeyed what the Bible said and was sensitive to the guiding of the Holy Spirit.

As a couple we desired to follow the Lord's instructions regarding training our children in His ways. Child rearing is not without challenges. Discipline is a great deal of work and often unpleasant. It is easier to just let children have their way and not require submission and obedience from them. I remember at times being too tired to deal with a situation properly, but I found that we all suffered from my lack of consistency, and then it took even more discipline to get things back on track.

The insights that Ab shares in this manual are from his heart. It is his desire to pass on a heritage of loving discipline to the generations that follow. Neither one of us had that kind of example in our own upbringing but by the Word of God and the power of the Holy Spirit, we have learned a better way. Not that we walked in it perfectly by any means, but we aspired to train our children in the ways of the Lord. With the breakdown of the traditional family structure and the watering down of moral principles within our society today, it is increasingly important to depend upon the Lord and His Word to guide and direct us that we might be salt and light in this fallen world. As you read this manual please know that it is written with much love and many prayers, not to condemn, but to impart wisdom through experience.

Sarah L. Sumrall

# INTRODUCTION

*"I have no greater joy than to hear that my children walk in truth."*

**III John v. 4**

Over the years this has become my life's verse. My desire is to see and hear that my children and grandchildren walk in the ways that are right and true. As Christian parents, we want to see our kids do well, be successful, and do better than we did when we were growing up. Truly, there is no greater delight for a parent than when others tell us of how the lives of our children have been an example and a blessing to them and to others.

After receiving my degree in education, teaching in the public schools for several years, serving for over twenty-five years in pastoral ministry, being married for over thirty years, raising my own family, and becoming a grandfather, I have personally observed first hand the need for a clear, concise Christian parent's manual on how we are to discipline our children in love.

Throughout my work with children, along with marriage and family counseling, I have come to realize that as God's children our ultimate goal should be that we, kids and parents alike, walk in truth. What is truth? Jesus said that He is the way, the truth, and the life and that no one comes to the Father but by Him (John 14:6).

As parents, we need to first walk in His truth so that we might say to our children, as the Apostle Paul said, "Follow me as I follow Christ" (1 Corinthians 11:1). This is the initial step in understanding Biblical discipline. Without being willing to walk in truth ourselves, we will never be able to properly teach and model truth for our children. The single most important decision that we can make is to first open our hearts and minds to God and His direction for our lives individually, so that we in turn can make wise choices for the overall well being of our entire family.

If you have never really made a decision to follow Christ, or perhaps you have but feel a need to renew that relationship, it's simply a matter of the heart. Being willing to acknowledge Him and say, "Lord I need your help. I believe that You love me, that You died for me, that You rose from the grave, and that You will live in and through my life as I yield my life to Your perfect will" (I Corinthians 15:3-4). It's that simple! God will meet you right were you are. He has promised us that if we draw near to Him, He will draw near to us (James 4:8). We can begin afresh and anew today! His mercies are new every morning! (Lamentations 3:22-23).

> *"Train up a child in the way he should go: and when he is old, he will not depart from it."*
>
> ### *Proverbs 22:6*

The Word of God clearly teaches that we are to train up our children in His ways. As we teach them to choose the right direction, when they are older, they will not stray from His ways. They will learn loving discipline and desire to remain steadfast in what they know to be right and true.

In light of the times in which we live, with political correctness being a driving force in our society, my desire is to pass on to my children, grandchildren, and their children a Biblical guide for loving discipline.

My prayer is that we, as parents, will have a hearing ear, an understanding heart, and a praying spirit. May we humbly submit our will to God's will for our lives and for the lives of our children. May we purposely and willfully choose to be obedient to His loving instructions.

Abner C. Sumrall

## CHAPTER 1

# WHAT IS LOVING DISCIPLINE?

*"For this is the love of God, that we keep his commandments: and his commandments are not grievous."*

**1 John 5:3**

There is a right way and a wrong way to administer correction. God's instructions are truly best for us. As a parent, loving discipline is not easy. Loving discipline is Biblical correction, which is not physical abuse. Physical abuse is not only unacceptable but also harmful, emotionally destructive, and against the law. Biblical correction, when administered in love, is always appropriate, helpful, encouraging, and honoring to God.

When I was a child my mom would often say, "You just wait until your dad gets home." I knew right away that I was in big trouble. At last, when my dad came home, after talking with my mom, he would tell me to go to my room and wait for him. In fear and trembling I would obediently go, knowing the dread that was to come. It seemed like an eternity before he finally came into my room. Then, he took off his belt and said, "Bend over, this is going to hurt me more than it hurts you." He whipped me in anger and between lashes, he asked, "Are you going to disobey your mother when she tells you to do something?" As the lashes continued he said, "Are you going to mind your mother from now on?" This continued until I cried out for mercy and promised that I would be good and obey. He then stomped out of the room and went his way while I lay there on my bed in tears—feeling bitter and resentful towards him. I could never figure out how it could hurt him more than it hurt me. That is, until I had my own children. Now I understand.

I don't blame my dad for his actions because he wasn't walking with God. He didn't read or understand the instructions that we have from God's Word or glean from the experiences and wisdom of others who desire to live in obedience to His ways.

We can learn from experience, but it doesn't have to be from our own experience. We can learn from the successes and failures of others. Too often we choose to raise our kids the way our parents raised us, or we decide to do just the opposite because we don't agree with the decisions that they made. The question is not what our parents did or didn't do, or what we think should or shouldn't be done, but what does God think? His Word declares that His commandments are not grievous (1 John 5:3). They are not extreme or outrageous, but they are best for us.

The story is told of the alcoholic father who went out one snowy night bundled up in his overcoat walking to the liquor store. After he had walked for a while, he heard a small voice calling out to him. He turned to see his six-year-old son following behind him, walking in his footprints. He realized that his little boy was following his footsteps to the liquor store. At that instant he had a revelation that his son was going to follow his example. From that moment on the father's life was radically changed.

What about us? Where are we leading our children? What kind of example are we setting for them to follow? Quite often our own kids are the ones who teach us. God uses our children to help us realize the importance of the life we are living. What is life really all about? Are we going to make life count? As parents, will we take seriously the Word of God and grasp hold of His promises? Will we realize the importance of being true to His Word and obedient to His instructions?

These challenging questions place an enormous responsibility upon us as parents to act in a loving, consistent manner towards our children just as our Heavenly Father does towards us. God is training us at the same time that we are training our children. I believe that God gives us children to help us grow up, mature, and to teach us His ways. Our relationship with our kids reveals our own spiritual maturity, or lack of development in our personal walk with God. We must evaluate our own life—the path we are taking—and realize that our kids are going to follow in our footsteps.

We can't really expect our kids to walk with God if we are not walking with Him. We are called to be an example in word and deed. The Bible tells us to be doers of the Word and not hearers only or else we deceive ourselves (James 1:22). It's not just what we say, but how we live our lives and the example we set on a daily basis.

Perhaps you can relate by way of your own story. Even now you may feel the guilt of knowing that you haven't been walking as close to God as you should. God doesn't condemn you. You may feel that you haven't been doing the best job in training your child correctly, or you have a desire to appropriately train your child and you are simply looking for a resource to lend a hand. Take hope! It's never too late or too early to simply choose to walk with the Lord and to learn how to correct your child in love.

Through the study of God's Word regarding discipline, my desire is not only to give you hope but also to give you step by step instructions of God's desire for you and your child concerning loving discipline.

Contained in this manual are seven steps to correcting your child in love. I have chosen the acronym RESPECT to help us Remember, Establish, Speak, Pray, Encourage, Correct, and Train. The Biblical principles behind each of these seven steps will be discovered throughout this book but will be discussed in greater detail in Chapter 13 – "Believing God's Word."

## Seven Steps to Correcting Your Child in Love

**RESPECT** – **R**emember, **E**stablish, **S**peak, **P**ray, **E**ncourage, **C**orrect, **T**rain

1. **R**emember to never lash out in anger! (James 1:20). Our anger does not bring about God's righteousness.

2. **E**stablish that God is love (1 John 4:8), and that God corrects those He loves (Hebrews 12:6). Because we love our children we discipline them (Ephesians 6:4).

3. **S**peak in a normal conversational tone. Speak the truth in love (Ephesians 4:15). Share what the Bible has to say about loving correction (Ephesians 6:1-2).

4. **P**ray without ceasing (1 Thessalonians 5:17). Praying always (Ephesians 6:18). From the moment correction is needed, continually ask for God's guidance and direction (James 1:5).

5. **E**ncourage one another (Hebrews 3:13). Support each other in loving obedience to God's Word.

6. Correct your child while there is hope (Proverbs 19:18; 29:17). Loving correction brings hope and peace (Romans 15:4).
7. Train up your child in God's ways (Proverbs 22:6).

These seven steps will not only develop mutual respect between parent and child but also increase our reverence and admiration for our loving Heavenly Father and His inspired Word.

You may be thinking that these principles sound reasonable but you are unsure as to how they work out practically in your own life and in raising your child. In Chapter 10 – "Discipline Develops Respect," each of these steps will be reviewed along with useful suggestions of how to implement them. Jesus said,

*"The things which are impossible with men are possible with God."*

*Luke 18:27*

It begins with you and with me. You are not alone! It's a choice that we make. This parent's manual is written with the hope that you will make the choice to realize that there is a better way. It's about training our children in the way they should go, which involves God's will for the direction we will choose for our lives and the example we will set for our children.

# CHAPTER 2

# OUR LOVING FATHER

*"… God is love."*

*1 John 4:8*

Too often our perception of our Heavenly Father is limited to our impressions and experiences, or lack thereof, with our earthly father. First of all, we must understand that God loves us and has a plan for our lives and for the lives of our children.

At times we all question and perhaps doubt God's love or His existence due to the circumstances or difficulties that come into our lives. If there is a God and if He is a God of love, then why does He allow evil to exist? What about 9/11, terrorism, the holocaust, child abuse, divorce, abortion, disabilities, sickness, disease, cancer, the death of a child or loved one? If God is a loving God then why does He allow evil and suffering to exist?

Many people have turned away from God because of these difficulties in life. Even the Biblical writers complained about suffering and evil:

> *"For innumerable evils have compassed me about..." (Psalms 40:12); "Why is my pain perpetual, and my wound incurable, which refuseth to be healed..." (Jeremiah 15:18); "... the whole creation groaneth and travaileth in pain together until now" (Romans 8: 22).*

The Bible reveals in the book of Genesis that in the very beginning of time God didn't create the world in the state in which it now exists. Evil came into being as a result of man's selfishness. His Word declares that God is a God of love. His desire was to create human beings who would willfully respond to His love. Truly, *"We love Him because He first loved us"* (1 John 4:19). Genuine love can't really exist unless it's freely given through the freedom of our own will. Mankind was given the choice to accept God's love or to reject it. Choosing to reject God's love brought evil into existence. When Adam and Eve disobeyed God, by their choice they brought evil into the world. *"God is good!"* (Psalms 73:1). God is not evil nor did He create evil. *"God is love!"* (1 John 4:8). Mankind brought evil upon himself by selfishly choosing his own way instead of God's ways.

> *"...by one man sin entered into the world..."*
> *Romans 5:12*

Because of Adam and Eve's sin, sickness, disease, and death entered into this world and now we suffer the universal consequences of their sin.

In the very beginning of time God created man to live forever, but because He is a sovereign God He allowed man to choose. Eve was deceived, but Adam willfully chose to disobey God. Because Adam bombed out—pun intended—we continue to suffer the repercussions and the fallout unto this day. God gives us a choice—to obey or disobey. He gives us the ability to say yes or no. He does not force Himself upon us.

The Bible tells us that it rains on the just and the unjust alike (Matthew 5:45). Christians face the same difficulties in life that unbelievers face. Jesus said that we would have tribulation in this world, but that we can be of good cheer because He has overcome the world (John 16:33). What do we do when trials and heartaches come our way? A wise man once said, "We can become bitter or we can become better." It is our choice! God can take the difficulties of this life and turn them around and use them for good. Just read the story of Joseph in the book of Genesis and you will be encouraged by God's faithfulness. What his brothers meant for evil in selling him into slavery, God used for good in promoting him to overseeing the land of Egypt and eventually saving the lives of his whole family. God's Word tells us that His purposes are sometimes beyond our understanding.

*"For my thoughts are not your thoughts, neither are your ways my ways, saith the Lord. For as the heavens are higher than the earth, so are my ways higher than your ways, and my thoughts than your thoughts."*

*Isaiah 55:8-9*

The Word of God informs us of how and why evil came about. We know that God is all wise and all knowing and that He has reasons for allowing things to happen that are beyond our comprehension.

God chose to make man in His own image. Yet, we are subject to trials, tribulations, hardships, and even death. God did not leave us to be destroyed. For God so loved you and me that He became a man and was tempted at all points (Hebrews 4:15). He willfully chose to experience the humanness of life, from the seemingly trivial difficulties of life to the worst humiliation, despair, suffering and death. But death was swallowed up in victory! He rose from the grave! He lives! (1 Corinthians 15:3-5). How do I know He lives? He lives within my heart. People can argue about doctrine or religion but they can't argue with how God has changed our lives.

Since the fall of man, we are all born with a sin nature and the persistence towards evil. So take heart and take hope, dear parent, God has not left you nor forsaken you. He loves you and desires the best for you and your precious family. He desires that you willfully choose to walk in His ways and to lead your child in the ways of God.

Now that we are reminded that there is a God, that He loves us, and that He wants what's best for us, certainly He wouldn't just leave this earth without giving us a plan for how to live our lives or how to raise our children in this fallen world. Surely He would equip us with an instruction manual, wouldn't He? Within the pages of this book you will not only discover God's loving instructions for Biblical discipline but also you will receive practical illustrations and applications of how to correct your child in love.

## CHAPTER 3

# FORGIVENESS BRINGS PEACE

*"Follow peace with all men, and holiness, without which no man shall see the Lord: Looking diligently lest any man fail of the grace of God; lest any root of bitterness springing up trouble you, and thereby many be defiled..."*

*Hebrews 12:14-15*

The Word of God declares that a root of bitterness will spring up and trouble us. What keeps springing up in our lives? What's causing us trouble? We wonder where in the world did that thought come from? Perhaps we assumed an issue was dealt with in the past, and yet here it is again. Most of us have had situations in our lives that were so painful and complex that we thought we could never forgive that person for what they have said or done.

A root of bitterness will spring up and bring difficulties into our lives. Bitterness will also infect and pollute others around us. For example, if we have a cut on our body that becomes infected, it will not only be a problem for us, but others may possibly be exposed to the infection, which could cause them harm as well. The infection must be removed in order for the wound to heal properly. Putting a bandage over it will only cover up the wound and allow the infection to still spread. This is why forgiveness is so very important. In order to dig up a root of bitterness we must choose to forgive. We forgive not because those who hurt or offended us deserve forgiveness, but because Jesus Himself, when He was on the cross looked down and said,

> *"Father forgive them for they know not what they do."*
>
> **Luke 23:34**

Certainly those who mocked Him, ridiculed Him, spit upon Him, and beat Him beyond recognition didn't deserve forgiveness. We may not feel like forgiving. Our Christian walk is not based on feelings, but upon faith in God. Feelings aren't necessarily right or wrong. It's what we do with those feelings. If we harbor bitterness in our hearts, it will not only trouble our lives but it will defile those around us: our spouse, our children, our relatives and our relationships with others. Forgiveness isn't just for the benefit of those being forgiven, but for the cleansing and restoration of those doing the forgiving as well.

Most of us are familiar with the Lord's Prayer:

*"After this manner therefore pray ye: Our Father which art in heaven, Hallowed be thy name. Thy kingdom come. Thy will be done in earth, as it is in heaven. Give us this day our daily bread. And forgive us our debts, as we forgive our debtors. And lead us not into temptation, but deliver us from evil: For thine is the kingdom, and the power, and the glory, forever. Amen."*

*Matthew 6: 9-13*

But many of us may not be familiar with what comes immediately following the Amen. In the following verses Jesus explains why forgiveness is so important:

> *"For if ye forgive men their trespasses, your heavenly Father will also forgive you: But if ye forgive not men their trespasses, neither will your Father forgive your trespasses."*
>
> *Matthew 6:14-15*

We must choose, in faith, to express forgiveness and receive forgiveness. It's a decision that we are compelled to make. If we harbor bitterness and resentment in our hearts, it will be like a wound that has become infected. It will bring difficulties upon ourselves and infect those around us in a negative way. We remove the bitterness by expressing and receiving forgiveness.

> *"But your iniquities have separated between you and your God, and your sins have hid his face from you, that he will not hear."*
>
> *Isaiah 59:2*

Sometimes we feel as if God isn't there, that He's not even listening to our prayers. He promises that

He will never leave or forsake us (Hebrews 13:5), but there are times when we have strayed and cut off intimate fellowship with Him by simply not recognizing sin and compromising in our walk.

When I was a child I would pray every night, "Forgive me of all of my sins." I didn't realize that when I had a bad attitude towards my mom, that it was sin. As I grew in my relationship with the Lord, I grew to understand the importance of identifying sin as anything that misses the mark, anything that displeases God. I began confessing specific sins to the Lord and no longer generalizing or lumping them all together.

If we can help our kids grasp and learn this concept as they grow and mature in their spiritual walk with the Lord, they will be light years ahead of most of us. As parents, we need to be willing to say, "Father, please forgive me for feeling bitter, hurt, and angry. Lord, I choose to forgive my child, my spouse, my brother, my friend, or my co-worker for what he or she said or did towards me." Most of us have had others in our lives who humiliated us. We can recall the specific incident of what they said or did that needs to be forgiven. Remember, our children are going to follow in our footsteps; so what kind of example are we setting?

When my children quarreled, I would have them look at each other and in faith say, "I'm sorry. Will you forgive me?" And the other respond, "I forgive you." They were learning to express forgiveness and receive forgiveness. Even when they didn't feel like forgiving, this first step would help to bring about reconciliation in their relationship. Instead of being angry, they began to convey love, acceptance, and friendship.

When we choose forgiveness, God brings a peace to our hearts and minds that surpasses our own understanding (Philippians 4:7). Truly, it's a God thing! It's by faith—not by sight or by feelings—that gives us the ability to forgive. It's faith in God to empower us to forgive. True, we don't forget and our enemy (Satan) is quick to remind us of our failures, but we simply agree with our adversary (Matthew 5:25). We recognize that without Jesus we are nothing, but in Him we can do all things through Christ who strengthens us (Philippians 4:13).

# CHAPTER 4

# LEARNING IN THE SANCTUARY

*"Until I went into the sanctuary of God; then understood I their end."*

**Psalm 73:17**

We can learn in the shelter of God's Word or we can learn through the storms and difficulties of life. How many times have we been driven to the Word of God because of the circumstances and situations that have come into our lives?

*"It is good for me that I have been afflicted; that I might learn thy statutes."*

**Psalms 119:71**

For many of us, when hard times come—when problems arise—that's when we hang on to the Lord and to the promises that He has given to us. We can look back and say that it's in our afflictions—during a time of distress—that we learn God's Word and the reality of how it applies to our lives personally. That's when God's Word becomes real to us. It isn't just words on the page. It isn't just hearing the Word. It's actually the Word being worked out in and through our lives.

*"Before I was afflicted I went astray: but now have I kept thy word."*

*Psalms 119:67*

Sometimes we can be doing the right things outwardly, but inwardly something is lacking. Years ago I fell eighteen feet off scaffolding and broke my ankle, leg, wrist and arm. It happened at a time when I was teaching the Word more than I ever had before in my entire life. I was also regularly attending Bible study, leadership meetings, worship, and communion services. Spiritually speaking, outwardly everything appeared that I was doing the right things.

After months of being crippled, I became discouraged and extremely frustrated. I began to pray, "Lord heal me or show me why I am not yet healed." It was in my affliction, during a time of crying out to the Lord, that He revealed a critical, judgmental spirit within my heart that needed to be recognized, dealt with and confessed unto Him. How much better would it have been had I learned in the sanctuary or at the communion table rather than in the storm of difficulty? But, it was in my affliction of brokenness and suffering that I heard and responded to the voice of the Lord.

*"For whom the Lord loveth he chasteneth, and scourgeth every son whom he receiveth."*

*Hebrews 12:6*

Truly, God chastens those whom He loves. Our Lord is more concerned about our spiritual, eternal state, than our present physical or emotional comfort in this life.

Again, He has promised that He will never leave us or forsake us (Hebrews 13:5). We can be thankful that our Lord is with us each and every step of the way, to guide, direct, and provide above and beyond what we could ask or think (Ephesians 3:20).

As he grows older, a child who has never been trained to discipline himself and bring his will into submission will require a great deal of correcting by the Lord. Because the Lord loves us, He chastens us all; but hopefully as we mature in our spiritual walk, less often do we have to endure His chastening ways. As we grow in our understanding of God and our obedience to Him, we have a greater desire not only to honor Him but also to bring Him pleasure.

After years of our own self-will and self-indulgence, God in His grace will chasten His children. Sometimes we end up going through greater sufferings simply because we are not obedient to His Word. How much better life will be for us if we will only submit our will to His.

> *"It is good for a man that he bear the yoke in his youth."*
>
> **Lamentations 3:27**

It is so much better for children to learn the ways that are right and true so that when they are older, they in turn will be able to teach their children the way they should go.

My mom was the one who took my sister and me to church. My dad worked rotating shifts at a mill and often slept during the day. He sometimes went to church on Christmas and Easter. I grew up wanting to know how old I had to be when I didn't have to go to church anymore. I wanted to stay home on Sunday nights with my dad and watch television. But my mom said, "As long as you live under the roof of this house, you're going to go to church." As soon as I graduated from high school I moved out and quit attending church. As I reflect on my life, I now understand that my mom's heart was right in training me in the ways of the Lord. She knew that she was doing her part, and knew that when I was older I would not depart. She knew that I would come back to my relationship with the Lord. She was right, because God's Word is true. We need to keep on keeping on! Do what we know is right!

In the Gospel of Mark people brought their young children to Jesus that He should touch them, but the disciples rebuked them. Jesus was displeased and said,

*"Suffer the little children to come unto me, and forbid them not..."*

**Mark 10:14**

He took the children up into His arms and put His hands upon them and blessed them. Christ displayed a gentle, compassionate attitude towards children.

Even though correction is unpleasant, do what the Word says! Follow the loving example of Jesus. Immediately after correction we can take our child, sit them on our lap, comfort, hold and kiss them. They may pull away because after having been disciplined, they may not feel like cuddling; however, we need to hold them, hug them, and express our love to them. It's part of the discipline process of correcting in love. This concept will be discussed in further detail in the remaining chapters.

*"Not forsaking the assembling of ourselves together..."*

**Hebrews 10:25**

Please note that we can learn either in the sanctuary where God's people gather or in the storms of life. As parents, it is so important that we regularly and consistently not only attend church but also take our children to church as well. Jesus said,

> *"For where two or three are gathered together in my name, there am I in the midst of them."*
> **Matthew 18:20**

God is faithful to meet us and teach us, to mold us and change us as we come together in His name. I can't begin to count the number of times God has spoken directly to my heart because I purposed to go to the sanctuary with Bible and notebook in hand, expecting to receive His guidance, direction and/or correction.

How about us, as parents? Are we regularly attending church? Are we teaching our kids by example what it means to walk with God—to wait upon Him—to worship Him—to pray to Him? Hey! Let's not feel guilty! Let's decide from this day forth, *"... as for me and my house, we will serve the Lord"* (Joshua 24:15).

## CHAPTER 5

# LOVE NEVER FAILS

*"For whom the Lord loveth he chasteneth, and scourgeth every son whom he receiveth. If ye endure chastening, God dealeth with you as with sons; for what son is he whom the father chasteneth not?"*

*Hebrews 12:6-7*

A selfish love always wants an easier way. Of course we can try to spare ourselves the pain of seeing our child endure suffering and disappointment, but we will then end up sending them out into the world totally unprepared for the natural consequences of life.

An unselfish love realizes that obedience must come at a cost and not without pain. God demonstrates His love to His children and He trains us through suffering. Jesus Himself endured the cross for us. He suffered for us. Perfection came through suffering (Hebrews 2:10).

We must seek the whole counsel of God. As we go through devotional times with our kids and deal with the issues of daily life, we must teach our kids how to think. They learn that there will be natural consequences resulting from the decisions they make. Quite often they will face consequences that are chastening. The consequences themselves are the correction.

When my son was attending preschool, once a week his class had a time of show and tell. He had received a ceramic bear bank that he wanted to share with his classmates. I explained to him that if he took the bank to school, it might possibly get broken. He responded, "Oh dad, please, can I take it?" I told him, "I just want you to know what the consequence may be. It could get broken." He decided to take it, and it got broken. I knew that this could very likely happen, but I let him make the decision. Did he get disciplined for that? No, the experience itself taught him that there are natural consequences for the decisions he makes in life.

If we defy the law of gravity and jump off a two-story building, we're probably going to get hurt. We know that there are natural consequences to our actions. If we allow our kids to suffer consequences regarding small decisions in life when they are young, how much better it will be for them as they grow older and deal with more important issues.

The purpose of loving correction is for children to learn cooperation, obedience and proper behavior. We are teaching and training our kids the right way to go while they are young so that when they are old—as the Word teaches—they will not depart from those ways and will be obedient to the Lord. The loving discipline that a child receives when he is young delivers him from negative character traits that, if uncorrected, may bring much greater suffering later in life.

> *"For all have sinned, and come short of the glory of God."*
>
> *Romans 3:23*

Yes, in the Greek, "all" means all. That includes all of us parents. We've all missed the mark. The Bible tells us that we were created for His pleasure (Revelation 4:11). When we displease Him in our thoughts, our actions, or our attitudes, we have sinned and displeased God.

We are all susceptible to stretching the truth or stating a fact but implying something else that really isn't true. One day when my daughter was attending elementary school, she arrived late. She was told to go to the office to get a tardy slip to take to her teacher. As she approached the office she was surprised to see a line of kids all waiting to get a tardy slip. The bus was late. Not just any bus, it was the bus she would have been riding had her mom not driven her to school. The great temptation was to say that the bus was late and her tardiness would have been excused. Right information, but it was the wrong implication. Yes, the bus was late. Yes, it was the bus she would have been riding had she ridden the bus that day. But she wasn't on the bus and that was not the reason she was late. She had a choice to make, and I'm proud to say that she told the truth even though the consequence was that she got an unexcused tardy.

*"…be sure your sin will find you out."*

**Number 32:23**

When my son was just a little guy, my wife baked a batch of fresh cookies. The aroma was breathtaking! He was given just one cookie and his mom told him not to have anymore. She went outside for a few minutes and then came back into the kitchen. Immediately she noticed that he looked a little suspicious, so she said, "Did you eat any more cookies?" The expression on his face revealed the answer. But he wondered, "How did she know?" The Word tells us to be sure that our sin will find us out (Numbers 32:23). He told the truth and admitted that he had eaten another cookie. She talked with him about what he had done wrong and how he had disobeyed, but thanked him for being truthful. Did he get disciplined for disobeying? No, because he readily admitted his mistake and confessed to his mom.

Confession is so important! Not just because we get caught but also because there is a cleansing effect that takes place through confessing our failings and receiving forgiveness. It's called grace: God's unearned, undeserved, unmerited favor. In this instance my son deserved and expected to be disciplined for disobeying, but he received his mom's loving grace because he was truthful. He confessed and asked for forgiveness for disobeying.

Truly God is good and His love never fails. As parents, we have no greater joy than to know that our children walk in truth (III John v. 4).

# CHAPTER 6

# CONSISTENCY IN FAITH

*"But without faith it is impossible to please him: for he that cometh to God must believe that he is, and that he is a rewarder of them that diligently seek him."*

**Hebrews 11:6**

*"So then faith cometh by hearing, and hearing by the word of God."*

**Romans 10:17**

It has been said that repetition is the key to learning. Throughout the book of Proverbs we find God's wisdom repeated. If God repeats His instructions, how much more do we need to be reminded of these

51

Biblical principles concerning how to lovingly discipline our children?

It's important that we are obedient to what the Word of God teaches and choose to discipline in a manner that is expressed in love. We can forget about the incident once the discipline is over. Then, fellowship is immediately restored with our children. We don't need to nag, scold, or become hostile. The child is lovingly disciplined. The problem is corrected. It's in the past.

Forgiveness is such an essential ingredient to the discipline process. As parents, we can't talk enough about the importance of forgiveness with our children, helping them understand their need to ask forgiveness for the wrong they have done. In faith, we choose to forgive them and together we ask the Lord's forgiveness, bathing the whole situation in prayer. The key is to receive forgiveness and to express forgiveness. In so doing, we realize that something is wrong and needs to be made right. Forgiveness is what makes our children appreciate loving correction. The anger and hostility that so often go along with disobedience diminish.

God commands us to consistently discipline our children even for the slightest willful disobedience.

Loving discipline should never be associated with anger or rejection. When our children deliberately refuse to obey, we chasten them in a patient, tender, and caring spirit. We do this out of loving obedience to God's instruction in His Word. Regardless of the circumstances and regardless of the offense when dealing with willful disobedience, the correction should always be the same; it should be like clockwork. Our children will then know what the consequence is because we have been consistent in training them. It's not lashing out in anger. When dealing with willful disobedience, loving correction brings hope.

My daughter, who is now an adult, was sharing her memories of how we disciplined her when we were visiting someone else's home. When she was disobedient I would say to her privately, "You're going to get a spanking when you get home." We didn't make a scene, we just calmly said, "You disobeyed." She was really quiet in the car on the drive home, hoping and praying that we might forget. We arrived home, had dinner and after reading devotions said, "Ok, it's time to go upstairs and get your spanking." Even though much time had past, we were consistent in following through which caused her to believe what we said.

Too often we naturally lash out in the flesh. Loving discipline is a decision that we make according to God's Word, out of obedience to what He desires. It's best for us and for our children. If we make that decision, God is going to strengthen us and see us through.

We need to help our children understand that Biblical correction is a gift of love by which they can receive the training God desires for them. Because of our love and concern, our children will then learn to receive the correction when they realize that its purpose is to lovingly train them. They begin to understand that we want to see them do well. We embrace them and show our affection in a way that resolves and dissolves pent up feelings.

Being trained in obedience as children prepares them to receive correction from God when they are grown. Even as parents the Lord chastens us because He loves us. Therefore, we need to judge ourselves (1 Corinthians 11:31). When we are disobedient in correcting our children, we need to be parents who are quick to say, "Lord forgive me." We should go to our children and ask their forgiveness. It's our responsibility to hear the Word, to obey the Word, and to train up our children in His ways. The result will be that they, too, will have a desire to honor and please Him.

*"Correction is grievous unto him that forsaketh the way: and he that hateth reproof shall die."*

*Proverbs 15:10*

To those who turn away from the ways of the Lord, severe discipline awaits them. Correction is very serious. But for those who walk in the way of the Lord, correction is a wonderful thing. It causes our mind to be fixed on things above — on the eternal things that really matter. Correction is not enjoyable, but it helps our hearts to be in tune with the heart of God and it molds us and makes us into His image.

## CHAPTER 7

# OUR TRAINING MANUAL

*"Train up a child in the way he should go: and when he is old, he will not depart from it."*

*Proverbs 22:6*

Today, our American culture is much too far away from what the Word of God teaches regarding the instruction and discipline of children. It is important that we return to the basics of what God's Word declares concerning how to train our children in His ways. We are losing the innocence of our children through the indoctrination of selfishness, greed, and pride, which leads to rebellion, disrespect for authority and casual and indiscriminate sexual behavior. Loving discipline, when practically applied, will not only make a difference in our society today, but also in the generations to come.

Correction begins in the home. The above scripture verse from the Book of Proverbs is a promise to all parents. My mom claimed this promise. In our household I was raised going to church, but I couldn't keep the rules and regulations of man's doctrine or the do's and don'ts of religion. There were plenty of well-meaning Christians always readily available to point out my shortcomings and misgivings; thus, I decided to live life my way. I willfully chose to walk away from the things of God and strayed for almost eleven years. When I called my mom to tell her that I had returned to the Lord, she said, "I knew that you would. I've been praying for you all these years, and the Lord promised that if I would train you up in His ways, when you were old you would not depart." She knew I would come back. She held on to God's promise.

May my mom's example be an encouragement to us as Christian parents. Perhaps a child is going his own way, doing his own thing and not walking in the ways of the Lord. We can take hope and hold on to the promises that God has given to us. If our children are still living at home, it is never too late for us to start doing what the Word declares by simply choosing to be obedient to His instructions. Jesus said,

> *"These things I have spoken unto you, that in me ye might have peace. In the world ye shall have tribulation: but be of good cheer, I have overcome the world."*
>
> *John 16:33*

Too often we are overwhelmed by difficulties in life and brought to the end of ourselves in frustration or disappointment. At times it is only when all else fails that we are willing to let the Lord take over and work in and through us. But we can choose today to say, "Lord, I want to be obedient to Your Word. My desire is to claim the promises that You have given to me, so that I might be able to see my children grow up in a way that would be honoring and pleasing in Your sight."

Regarding the training of our children, we are wise to be completely dependent on the Lord. Truly, our children are a gift, given to us for a season. But we need to give our children back to the Lord. We have the responsibility to train them up and then to let them go. We need to know how to do this properly. We need instructions. We need an instruction manual.

Indeed we have a manual, "Emanuel"—God with us. He has given us the Bible—His Holy Word—so that we are able to say, "This is how to do it! This is how to train up our children in the way they should go." Many of us teach our children the best way we know how, but are we neglecting to teach them and train them in the way that is right and true according to the Word of God?

A child can be trained to respond to his parents in obedience and in trust. The definition of the word "train" in the Hebrew text is "to narrow, to initiate or discipline, dedicate, train up." (Strong) In our English language the definition is "to mold the character, to instruct by exercise, drill, to make obedient to orders, to put or point in that direction, to prepare for the contest." (Webster) These definitions contain exactly what God would have for us regarding the training of our children.

Today, there are those in our society who are attempting to change the meaning of words in our English language. For example, there are some special interest groups that desire to redefine the word "marriage." Webster's Dictionary, copyright 1976, defines marriage as "the mutual relation of husband and wife; the institution whereby men and women are joined in a special kind of social and legal dependence for the purpose of founding and maintaining a family." (Webster) If you look at a more recent edition, you will not find that definition. It doesn't mention men or women. It simply states, "domestic partners." Is marriage really a contract between one man and one woman? We can turn to the Word of God and find the answer to that question. It is especially important that we constantly seek God's Word for divinely inspired direction. We can look at life through the lens of Scripture, allowing His Holy Spirit to instruct us in how to live. Truly His Word is a light to our path and a lamp to our feet (Psalm 119:105).

*"If any of you lack wisdom, let him ask of God, that giveth to all men liberally, and upbraideth not; and it shall be given him."*
*James 1:5*

The subject of discipline and correction according to Biblical principles is not considered to be politically correct. But what we must do is pray and ask God to show us what His Word proclaims. He tells us if we lack wisdom and need understanding to simply ask, and He will generously give it to us. His Word will last forever. He never changes. He is the same yesterday and today (Hebrews 13:8). He has given us His Word and His commandments are not grievous (1 John 5:3). They are best for us. His desire is that we walk in these truths. Why? Because it will be good. Good for us. Good for our kids. Good for those around us.

*"Trust in the LORD with all thine heart; and lean not unto thine own understanding. In all thy ways acknowledge Him, and He shall direct thy paths."*

*Proverb 3:5*

Most of us, in raising our children, will either deliberately or unconsciously train them in God's way or by our own impulses. When we ask one of our children to do something, are we training them to wait until we have asked them twice or maybe three times before they obey? Are we training them to wait until we have raised our voice? How many times do we have to ask and how high or how loud does our voice need to be raised before we really expect them to obey? Are we training them to wait until we threaten them before they obey?

We can train our children to obey immediately, asking them just once in a normal conversational tone. But, I should add, this is not something that takes place in our natural, human tendency. This is a God thing—a spiritual discipline that we need the empowering of the Holy Spirit to help us accomplish.

Sometimes our children can push our buttons and get under our skin. This causes us to say and do things we regret. We need the power of the Holy Spirit and the instruction from the Word of God to avoid getting into a battle of us against them.

Many of us relate to the frustration of a parent attempting to discipline their child in a public setting, perhaps in a department store or a grocery store. The child starts throwing a temper tantrum. The parent, after calmly trying to persuade the child to behave to no avail, starts losing control. Anger begins to flare up, the tone of voice rises, and it quickly becomes quite a scene. In trying to discipline the child the parent is humiliated. Both parent and child appear foolish and immature.

As we look to the Scriptures, we can distinguish whether or not we are being obedient to God's Word as parents, so that we might then train our children to be obedient to us. A child, who has only been told the way that he should go but not disciplined, can be easily influenced to go astray from what is right and true.

As parents we are given the promise that those who train their children in the Lord, that when the child is old, he will not depart from it. What a wonderful promise to us as parents! If we train our children now, when they are older they are going to live their lives according to the principles and precepts set forth in God's Word. They are going to know and hopefully choose to do what is right.

## CHAPTER 8

# HOW DO WE TRAIN?

*"Obey them that have the rule over you, and submit ourselves..."*

**Hebrews 13:17**

*"Likewise, ye younger, submit yourselves unto the elder..."*

**1 Peter 5:5**

During my son's junior high school years he and I enrolled in karate classes with a Christian instructor who attended our church. It was a great time for a father and son to spend time hanging out and learning together. We not only learned a new sport, but through the martial arts we also learned discipline and respect for authority. Instruction, dedication, exercise and drills were molding our character. All of this was in preparation for advancement in the various ranks and degrees of proficiency. It wasn't easy and it took a lot of hard work. Most successful athletes, regardless of the sport, in preparing for competition have a planned, disciplined program of appropriate training.

In the previous chapter we looked at the meaning of the word "train" in the Hebrew and English languages. We must not lose sight of these definitions, "to train up, to initiate, discipline, dedicate, to mold the character, to instruct by exercise, drill, to make obedient to your request, to put and point in the right direction, to prepare for the contest."

As we look at life through the lens of Scripture, let's take a look at two Biblical models. In the first example the child is "trained" in the way he ought to go. In the second illustration the children are shown the way, but not "trained."

In the Old Testament we see that when Hannah prayed she asked the Lord for a son and promised to give him back to the Lord.

*"And she vowed a vow, and said, O LORD of hosts, if thou wilt indeed look on the afflic-*

*tion of thine handmaid, and remember me,
and not forget thine handmaid, but wilt give
unto thine handmaid a man child, then I
will give him unto the LORD all the days of
his life, and there shall no razor come upon
his head."*

*1 Samuel 1:11*

Notice Hannah didn't say, "Lord, if you give me a son I will do my best to teach him to serve You. If he is willing and doesn't object, then I'll take him up to the temple to serve You." She never doubted that her son would do anything other than what she chose for him.

*"For this child I prayed; and the LORD
hath given me my petition which I asked of
him: Therefore also I have lent him to the
LORD; as long as he liveth he shall be lent
to the LORD. And he worshipped the LORD
there."*

*1 Samuel 1:27*

Hannah led her son Samuel to the temple. He was a willing servant to Eli the priest. It is evident in the

Book of I Samuel that as a young boy, Samuel had been trained to obey. Three times he heard a voice in the night and got out of bed and ran to Eli asking him what he wanted. It was the Lord speaking to him, and Samuel responded immediately in obedience.

In the second example we see the two sons of Eli the priest.

*"Now the sons of Eli were sons of Belial; they knew not the LORD."*

*1 Samuel 2:12*

Scripture reveals how Eli's sons were disobedient and immoral. Eli knew what his sons were doing and he scolded them. As their father, he no doubt told them what was right.

*"And he said unto them, Why do ye such things? for I hear of your evil dealings by all this people. Nay, my sons; for it is no good report that I hear: ye make the LORD'S people to transgress... they hearkened not unto the voice of their father..."*

*1 Samuel 2:23-25*

Please take note; scolding is not "training." Eli neglected to train his sons; therefore, they did not listen to or obey their father or the Lord. As a result, the Lord cut off future generations of Eli's descendants from the priesthood.

*"For I have told him that I will judge his house forever for the iniquity which he knoweth; because his sons made themselves vile, and he restrained them not."*

*1 Samuel 3:13*

According to God's Word, Eli's sons were despicable. In his lack of discipline, Eli honored his sons above the Lord. He loved the Lord and was sincere as he performed the office of a priest, but he was sincerely wrong in not training his sons to obey.

What a lesson for us in learning the importance of training our children in the way they should go. It's not just teaching them the way, pointing to the way, or telling them about the way, but training them in the way. We are preparing to thrust them out into the world, and they need to be ready to stand firm upon the foundation of what is right and true.

When I was teaching elementary school, I didn't just tell the students to go down the hall, turn right, follow the hallway past five classrooms, turn left, go past the front office, and the library would be the first door to their right. No! They would all line up in an orderly fashion, and I would show them the way. They followed my example until they learned the way.

The question that every parent encounters is "How can we train our children to obey us?" God has given us the answer. It's in His Word—the Word of God—the Bible. We are given specific instructions in how to train our children to be successful in life.

## CHAPTER 9

# UNDERSTANDING THE NEED FOR CORRECTION

*"I will instruct thee and teach thee in the way which thou shalt go: I will guide thee with mine eye. Be ye not as the horse, or as the mule, which have no understanding: whose mouth must be held in with bit and bridle, lest they come near unto thee."*

*Psalm 32:8-9*

How does this translate for us? In a sense, God is saying this is the type of sensitivity and response toward Him that we should desire for our lives. Not as a mule with no understanding needing to be jerked about from one direction to another, but a heart that is submitted to God. We must decide to obey His Word, and then we seek His guidance. We ought to pray for the obedience that we ourselves need in order to affectively discipline our children.

> *"Behold, we put bits in the horses' mouths, that they may obey us; and we turn about their whole body."*
>
> *James 3:3*

As a young adult, I owned a horse named Trouble. His name alone should tell you a little about his nature. Believe me, he was a lot of trouble. When I rode him, I would get blisters on my hands from pulling back on the reigns just trying to get him to stop. He would not obey my commands or listen to my instruction regardless of how loud I would yell—"Whoooaa!!!"

I met a young lady who was selling her bridle and saddle. She encouraged me to try the bridle and bit just to see if they would make a difference. The bit alone radically changed my horse's personality. He was no longer any trouble at all. He responded immediately to every tug on the reigns.

So, too, for us as parents it's the "rod of correction" that's going to make the difference in training our children in the ways of the Lord. When lovingly applied, it will change their personality from the rebelliousness of their sin nature to a character that will be honoring and pleasing to God and to us, as parents.

*"Foolishness is bound in the heart of a child; but the rod of correction shall drive it far from him."*

*Proverbs 22:15*

During the formative years of our children's lives, we kept an oak paddle in a special place in our home. This "rod of correction" was a constant reminder of the consequences of willful disobedience. It was professionally made, stained, and finished with the verse from Proverbs 22:15 written in calligraphy on its side. It worked exceptionally well. Correction comes from consistent, loving discipline.

Our children are now grown but are appreciative of the "rod of correction" in their developing years. They are grateful that much foolishness had been driven from their lives by consistent loving discipline. The oak paddle didn't just sting; it hurt! It was character building and made an obvious difference. It was the rod that we needed. We realized that a spanking needed to hurt. Why? If it doesn't hurt, it doesn't work. Please do not misunderstand; I am not in any way encouraging physical abuse, but rather advocating loving, firm, consistent, Biblical correction.

In December of 2007, *Family News in Focus* published an on-line article entitled "American College of Pediatricians Supports Spanking." (ACP) The basis of the article and the research reveals that doctors say reasoning and explanation do not work with young children. Their research finds that spanking "can be a useful and necessary part of a successful disciplinary plan." (FNIF)

The principal author of the report, Den A. Trumbull, MD, FCP said: "Spanking is, at times, necessary with young children because reasoning and explanation are insufficient in persuading them to have good behavior. Spanking should be used proactively. The child should be forewarned; it should be administered in private, and followed by a loving embrace of the child with an explanation for the reason of the spanking." (FNIF)

The American College of Pediatricians offers more information online at their website: www. ACPeds.org. The research is entitled, "Discipline of the Child, Corporal Punishment: A Scientific Review of its Use in Discipline," by The American College of Pediatricians.

It is reassuring to know that current research reveals what the Bible has been saying all along. As Christians, we must continually look at the Law of the Lord, God's Word, and be obedient and consistent in disciplining our children in love. If our Heavenly Father loves us and chastens those whom He loves, should we not follow His example, as earthly parents, and correct our children in love?

We think, "Oh, but I just love little Johnny too much. I don't want to hurt him." Really?

*"He that spareth his rod hateth his son: but he that loveth him chasteneth him betimes."*

*Proverbs 13:24*

If you spare the rod, you will definitely spoil your child. The Word is very clear on this subject. If you spare the rod, the Bible says you hate your child, but if you love him you will be diligent to discipline him.

In the days and times in which we live, we are told that there are other ways in which we can discipline. We can redirect their energy into a more positive direction. Really? Where does it say that in the Bible? We must turn to the Word of God and receive our instructions from Him. The Lord declares that His thoughts are not our thoughts and neither are our ways His ways (Isaiah 55:8). We may use scolding and try to give an excuse as to why it should be used in place of the rod. Much too often, we try to justify ourselves and make the Scriptures conform to what we feel or think, but it is evident that His ways and His thoughts are much higher than ours.

If we look up the meaning of the word "rod," in the Hebrew, we will find that the definition is not using words to reason, but "literally, a stick for punishing, fighting, ruling, walking, or figuratively, correction, rod, a scepter or staff." (Strong) In Biblical times a shepherd's staff was used for protecting the sheep as well as caring for and correcting them.

The rod of correction is an instrument that works to drive away foolishness. When our children were in their early developmental stages—one to five years of age—we had an oak paddle in our home and wooden dowels in each of our cars. We were always prepared. We were ready to immediately deal with a situation to help them understand the consequence of their willful disobedience.

***"Withhold not correction from the child: for
if thou beatest him with the rod, he shall not
die. Thou shalt beat him with the rod, and
shalt deliver his soul from hell."***

***Proverbs 23:13-14***

We are literally delivering our children from hell
by properly using the rod of correction. This loving
correction changes and molds their character to teach
them how to obey, to learn respect, and to appreciate
Godly discipline.

When my son was preschool age, I was preparing
to teach a Bible study concerning the reality of hell.
While in the midst of looking up the word "hell,"
being described as a place of outer darkness and
eternal separation from God, my son walked in.

"Dad, what are you doing?"

"I'm studying."

"What are you studying?"

I began to explain to him what the Scriptures
teach concerning hell, when suddenly I thought of an
illustration that might help him better understand. I
took him into our bathroom, closed the door, turned
off the light, and spun him around and around, and
then backed away against the wall.

After a few seconds of silence, I heard his little voice, "Da...a...a...ddy!" In the darkness, feeling a little disoriented, he had lost perspective of my presence, the direction of the door, or the position of the light switch. Of course I immediately turned on the light and gave him a big hug and held him and loved on him. At that moment, I began to explain to him how, in hell, people would be separated from God—our Heavenly Father—just as he was separated from me. In outer darkness they will be disoriented and not have perception of direction just like he had lost his bearings, but they will be lost forever. Again, it was an opportunity to lovingly reiterate what the Scripture teaches—the consequences of not using the rod of correction—hell itself—and why we should be obedient to God's Word.

We then talked about the importance of Heaven, the Gospel message of God's love, and His desire that none should perish but that all come to the knowledge of the truth (1 Timothy 2:4). God's desire is that we be in Heaven with Him forever (John 3:16).

## CHAPTER 10

# DISCIPLINE
# DEVELOPS RESPECT

*"The rod and reproof give wisdom: but a child left to himself bringeth his mother to shame."*

*Proverbs 29:15*

The wisdom that comes from reprimanding with the rod brings forth correction. One might think, "But my child is just so young and still in diapers." With our kids we discovered that it was ineffective to spank through a diaper. Again, if it doesn't hurt, it doesn't work. We would pull the diaper down and strike them with the rod of correction, right on their bare bottom. Some might say, "I'll wait until they are a bit older so that I can reason with them and then they will understand." Even the research from The American College of Pediatricians disagrees with this theory.

How many times have we observed a parent with their child? As they become older, they learn to crawl, walk, and run. Then they may bolt away at the most inopportune time with the parent yelling, "Stop!" at the top of their lungs. As the Word declares, it brings shame, humiliation and embarrassment to have a child who willfully disobeys. But even more importantly there is a concern for the safety of a child who is left on his own to decide whether or not to cooperate. We are responsible to teach our child to respond in obedience. Do we let our child decide whether to stick his finger in the electrical outlet or touch the hot stove? Of course not! I wonder how many trying incidences could be avoided through consistent loving discipline. Always remember and never forget that the motive is not about control, but it is all about love. Loving God so much that you desire to be obedient to His Word, and loving your child enough to be willing to consistently correct your child in love.

*"Chasten thy son while there is hope, and let not thy soul spare for his crying."*
**Proverbs 19:18**

Correct them while there is hope! Consistent discipline of our children will make a difference in their lives as well as ours. As they are growing and maturing, they are coming to know the love of God, the goodness of God, and the discipline of God through us, as their parents. Just as the Lord is Lord over our lives, He has ordained us to be the authority over our children as long as they are living in our home. It is our God ordained responsibility to train them.

*"Correct thy son, and he shall give thee rest; yea, he shall give delight unto thy soul."*
**Proverbs 29:17**

Throughout the book of Proverbs and all through the Scriptures, we are told to chasten and correct our children with the rod and with reproof, withholding not correction. We should not really argue with the Word of God and yet sometimes we do just that. It's not an easy request to carry out. We don't want to spank our children. We will try anything but spanking, but the Word is clear on how we need to discipline our children.

The question is, "Do we believe God and what He says in His Word?" We love our kids and we want to obey God; therefore, we must take up the rod and physically spank them when they disobey. As tough and difficult as it might be, we choose to remain in control and not lash out in anger or frustration. By faith we obey His Word. We allow God to fulfill the promise that He has given concerning raising our children in His ways.

It's so easy for us to come up with excuses. As I reflect back over the years and the multitude of times when it was much easier to say, "He's too tired or she didn't get a nap today, or he hasn't been feeling well." All of these were really excuses for my disobedience to God's Word. Please don't misunderstand, as parents we need to provide structure, encourage naps, proper nutrition, and limit the amount of sugar intake to help our children to be able to obey. Otherwise they will be bouncing off the walls, and we will be feeling overwhelmed.

As we go through the Scriptures, we do not read, "Chasten your son only when he is well rested."

We must be diligent to do what the Word says. Our obedience to God in lovingly training our children requires that every time we ask them to do something, whether it is to come to us or not to touch something, to be quiet or to put something down; regardless of what it is, even in the seemingly most insignificant request, it's our responsibility to train them to obey. We just say it once in a normal winsome tone. We don't need to raise our voice, shout, scream, threaten, or count to five before they will obey. If we do, we are teaching them that we don't really mean what we say until the tone of our voice is raised or until we begin counting. If they are disobedient to our request or don't respond but ignore us, we simply implement the seven steps to correcting our child in love. These seven steps, along with the scriptural references are reprinted in Appendix B – "Parent's Checklist."

This is an exceptionally significant concept. When we discipline our child in love, we develop mutual respect. Not only respect for God and His authority, but respect for one another as a parent and child. Again, that's why I've chosen the acronym RESPECT – Remember, Establish, Speak, Pray, Encourage, Correct, and Train. As a teacher, statistics reveal that the key to learning is repetition. This review of the following seven steps of correcting your child in love contain practical suggestions when it comes to appropriate discipline:

Remember to never lash out in anger! We wait for our emotions to calm down. If necessary, in our own mind, under our breath, count to ten or to one hundred and ten, or send them to their room to wait for a while.

Establish God's love. Remind our kids and our self that God chastens those He loves and because we love them, we correct them.

Speak in a normal, conversational tone. Take the time to explain what the Bible — the Word of God — clearly teaches concerning correction. Also let our kids know that we need to be obedient to the Lord in training them in His ways, according to the instructions given to us in God's Word.

Pray! Ask for God's guidance and direction throughout the discipline process. Pray always with expectation that God not only hears our prayers, but answers them.

Encourage one another. Support each other in loving obedience to God's Word. Physically open the Bible and show our children the Scriptures and read the verses aloud. It's not a battle of us against them!

It's a matter of being obedient to a loving God who desires the best for us and for our child.

Sit, listen, and encourage them to talk about what they have done wrong and why he or she is going to get a spanking. Ask, "What did you do wrong?" Let them answer. Help them think through what they have done. "Why are you getting a spanking?" Help them understand why and repeat the Scriptures.

Correct our child while there is hope. Loving correction brings hope and peace. Bend them over our knee and spank them with a rod, not with our hand. Keep in mind; we want them to fear the rod and to love us. Hug them, pray with them, and love on them. Tell them how much we love them and care about them.

Train our child in God's ways. "What do you say to Mommy (or Daddy)?" Teach them to say, "I'm sorry, will you forgive me?" Then respond, "I forgive you! Now let's ask God to forgive you also." Teach them to pray. A simple prayer is, "Dear Jesus, please forgive me for disobeying Mommy (or Daddy). Help me to be a good boy (or girl) and learn to obey." Now, it's over and done with. The correction releases the guilt and relieves all those pent up feelings. We are able to love, embrace, express and receive forgiveness and press on. We will look at these seven steps in even greater detail in Chapter 13 – "Believing God's Word."

It is imperative that as parents we test the rod on ourselves to know how far to draw back in order to be effective but not abusive. We do not want to inflict injury! Remember, we want to break their will without breaking their spirit. With my children it was five swats. In Biblical numerology five is the number of grace. Grace is God's undeserved, unearned, unmerited favor. My children knew when that time came they were expected to go upstairs, bend over my knee, and receive five good hard swats. It changed their lives in a radical way and it strengthened the relationships within our family. Loving discipline brought peace and tranquility to our home.

There are times when we might lose our temper but we must not lash out in anger. Believe me, everyone will pay for it! I can remember one experience in particular when my son was just a toddler. We were wrestling around on the floor when he suddenly bit me on the inside of my thigh. I reacted in a way that surprised him as much or more than it surprised me. Without thinking, I immediately grabbed a hairbrush from the bedroom dresser, turned him over my knee, and gave him five good swats. Even though the back of the hairbrush didn't carry the sting of the oak paddle, it was upsetting for him. Why? First of all, I did not follow the Biblical model of correcting him in love to which he had been accustomed. Secondly, I reacted so quickly that he did not see the hairbrush and thought that I had hit him with my hand. He had been trained to fear the rod and to love and respect me.

We all make mistakes but that is no excuse to justify our actions in lashing out in anger. If we do, we risk inflicting injury upon our child, which is never our intention. Our purpose is to lovingly and patiently maintain discipline and promote the overall welfare of our child. We may at times react and say or do things that we regret. This was one of those times for me. Later, I went back to him, confessed and asked him to forgive me for acting inappropriately. Then, once again, I explained to him what the Bible teaches about the rod of correction and how we should properly deal with these issues.

As adults, it is incredibly difficult to humble ourselves enough to apologize to a pre-schooler, yet it shows our child that we love them and respect them as well. It reveals our love for the Lord and our desire to not only reverence Him, but also to be obedient to His Word.

A number of times over the years I went to my children and asked their forgiveness for not being obedient to God's Word and diligent in disciplining them in the way that I should, particularly when I let things slide and hadn't spanked them when they needed it. When I would ask their forgiveness, they would look at me as if I were crazy. Teaching our children the principles of expressing and receiving forgiveness is as necessary for us, as parents, as it is for our kids.

## CHAPTER 11

# ENCOURAGE
# ONE ANOTHER

*"But exhort one another daily, while it is called today; lest any of you be hardened through the deceitfulness of sin."*

*Hebrews 3:13*

We should encourage one another each and every day concerning the truth that God has revealed to us in His Word. We must decide to remind each other of the significance of correcting our child in love and using the rod of correction in disciplining our children in obedience to the Word of God.

Many times we come up with excuses and reasons to compromise. We say, "Isn't every child different?" Yes, it's true that we need to look at each individual personality, but we all have one thing in common. We are all born with a sin nature. We don't need to teach our kids to disobey. They instinctively already know how. Each child needs the rod to bring them to a place of obedience and submission.

Nowhere do we see in Scripture God qualifying His command on the basis of personality, although, that is our tendency. Little Johnny is like this, so we need to take a time out. When it came to disciplining my own children, I didn't see "time out" in the Word. Now that I have grandchildren, I am rethinking and relearning this concept. His Word tells us to be still and know that He is God (Psalm 46:10). Also, to be quick to listen, slow to speak, and slow to anger (James 1:19). The word "Selah" appears often in the Psalms, which means to pause, to stop, and think about it. As a grandparent, I am now finding it helpful for everyone to take a time out. Usually one minute for each year of the child's age. For my grandson that would be four minutes sitting in the corner, pausing, stopping, and thinking. (For grandpa, it would be fifty-nine minutes!) It's a time that he can think about why he is being punished and what would happen if he continued to willfully disobey. He has learned that when he disobeys his grandparents, he will be in big trouble with his mom and dad. (Please note that time out is not an effective replacement for spanking—only a deterrent.) Following the time out we then come back together for a time of confession, asking forgiveness, receiving forgiveness, and expressing forgiveness. As we go through the Scriptures, God's Word clearly gives us His instructions. We should simply be obedient to His Holy Spirit.

> *"Can two walk together, except they be agreed?"*
>
> *Amos 3:3*

Mom and Dad, the key to effective discipline is that you agree on what the Scriptures teach and discuss the importance of being consistent and diligent. We have all heard of parents who have inappropriately administered correction in a way that is not Biblical. If we are not in agreement concerning how to discipline, the enemy will use that to drive a wedge between us. Our child will use our disagreement to play us against each other. We should be those who desire to lovingly discipline our children, consistently in unison as mom and dad, not allowing our flesh to lash out in anger.

During the formative years of our children's lives, my wife and I desired to deal with every issue of willful disobedience by using the rod of correction. Every little temper-tantrum, act of defiance, or talking back with an attitude was basically requesting a spanking. I would say to my daughter, "Look in my eyes. You change your attitude or I'll change it for you." She would respond, "I'll change my attitude Daddy! I'll change my attitude!" Why? She did not want the rod of correction applied to the seat of learning. She knew how it felt. She knew that it would hurt.

That's our goal! We point to the rod as a reminder, and it does its job. Eventually we don't need to use the rod because we have been consistent. We have been diligent in doing what God has asked of us and our child has learned loving obedience.

It's similar to when we are driving down a steep hill and we find ourselves going a little faster than the posted speed limit. We look ahead and notice a police car waiting on the side of the road. What's our automatic response? We gear down, tap the brakes, and slow down. Now, why do we do that? It's because we have learned to respect the police as a position of authority. We also recognize the possible consequences of disobeying the posted speed limit.

Just as we react to the police car, our children will learn to respect the rod of correction and respond in a way that will be right and pleasing in God's sight and ours. This also allows the rod to represent itself as a disciplinary tool allowing our child to fear it and not us, but still respect that we, as parents, hold the authority and power to the rod.

In my son's own words, "As a kid the paddle creped me out even when I just saw it when I wasn't in trouble. It personified itself with the discipline. It was okay for me to dislike the paddle because it kept me from disliking my parents for the discipline."

# CHAPTER 12

# RECEIVING GOD'S GUIDANCE

*"But be ye doers of the word, and not hearers only, deceiving your own selves."*

***James 1:22***

The question often arises, "How many times a day do we need to discipline our children? They continually disobey. We've asked them to cooperate and they refuse to comply." The Word encourages us to be consistent, each and every time. As the old Nike advertising campaign would say, "Just do it!" Faith comes by hearing and hearing by the Word of God (Romans 10:17). We are not to be those who just hear the Word, but those who purpose in our hearts to do what the Word tells us.

"Are we going to break their spirit?" No, with proper discipline, we are going to break their will, but not break their spirit. This requires faith on our part to obey the Lord as He has so graciously instructed us through His Word. God is going to teach our kids to be subject to our authority as we are subject to His authority. Discipline will influence our children positively in their personality and instill within them Godly character. Our obedience will bring about a disciplined spirit within our children that frees them to blossom to their fullest capacity. They need not be swayed by the circumstances of life or the situations that will transpire in their lives. Jesus said,

*"...every branch that beareth fruit, he purgeth it, that it may bring forth more fruit."*

*John 15:2*

In the spring season, we observe the fruit trees that have been pruned and witness the beauty of the buds blossoming forth. That's what happens when a vine is pruned. It flourishes and bears fruit. So, too, with our kids when we prune them with loving discipline, using the rod, they will flourish and do well.

Correction will bring forth fruit in their lives and in their personalities. Loving discipline develops positive character traits that can only come about through chastening.

As parents, God is training us also. Correction is part of what we will continue to endure until He takes us to be with Him. Our relationship with our children should be a picture of the relationship that we have with our Heavenly Father, our God and Friend. We desire for Him to be the Lord of our lives. When our kids live in our home, we are placed in charge over them by the Lord to train them to know that there is a loving God who desires to be the Lord of their lives also.

*"Obey them that have the rule over you, and submit yourselves..."*

*Hebrews 13:7*

Most of us at some point in our lives have had a landlord. The landlord tells us whether or not we can have a pet and informs us of expectations while living in the rental. We have also had various employers who have authority over us in the work place. We all learn submission in one way or another. It's God's ordained plan for our children to learn submission, so that when they have others overseeing them, they are able to respectfully submit and honor those positions of authority. If a child never learns discipline and submission, in an adult world the consequences can be life changing and dramatic.

When God chastens us, His action towards us is for our own good. It's not God out to get us, or zap us, for doing wrong. It's because He loves us; He corrects us.

*"O that there were such an heart in them, that they would fear me, and keep all my commandments always, that it might be well with them, and with their children for ever!"*

*Deuteronomy 5:29*

That's what God desires of us. That we would have a heart to not only fear Him, but to also reverence and honor Him. His heart is that we keep His commandments so that it will be well with us. It will be good for us, and also it will be best for our kids. This is the same heart and attitude we need to have with our kids.

**"For they verily for a few days chastened us after their own pleasure; but he for our profit, that we might be partakers of his holiness..."**

**Hebrews 12:10**

God loves us and He cares about us. As parents, we are going to continue to receive His loving discipline. When my kids were rude or talked back to their mom or to me, my natural tendency, in my flesh, was to feel offended. I just couldn't believe that they would say or do something like that.

**"And, ye fathers, provoke not your children to wrath: but bring them up in the nurture and admonition of the Lord."**

**Ephesians 6:4**

We need to be the mature adults. We need to be the parents. Our tendency is to react in the same immature way that our child is acting towards us. We need the Holy Spirit to help us to choose what we know is right. In love for our child and in obedience to God, we take up the rod and patiently correct them. We put them on our lap. We love them and tell them what they have done wrong. We talk about it. We teach them to verbalize what they did wrong and why it's wrong. We explain the consequences of doing wrong and then we spank them. Afterwards, we embrace them and encourage them to ask not only for God's forgiveness, but also for our forgiveness as well. We bask in forgiveness. We receive forgiveness, and we express forgiveness. This important concept cannot be emphasized enough. If it's not done in love, our kids will rebel. They will feel bitter, and we end up provoking them to anger.

It is so essential that all of these things be done in love. If we are faithful to train up our children, and to bring them into submission to our will, then as they grow older they will transfer that same submission to God. They will learn to take the Word of God seriously. As they go—as they grow—and as they become more mature in the ways of the Lord, they will realize that our desire to train them in His ways is simply out of our obedience to God's will. It's because we love our kids, we love God, and we desire to honor the Lord and bring Him pleasure.

*"...the spirit is willing, but the flesh is weak."*
*Matthew 26:41*

*"...walk in the Spirit so that you do not carry out the desires of the flesh."*

**Galatians 5:16**

Spiritually, we can all agree with what we know to be right and true according to God's Word. Yet, physically and emotionally it's our natural human tendency to lash out in the flesh and respond in a way that is inappropriate. Initially, perhaps it would be helpful to make a discipline checklist. Am I: Angry? Acting In Love? Speaking in a normal tone? Praying? Encouraging? Using a rod? Training appropriately? (Please note Appendix B - Parent's Checklist)

It is so crucial for us as parents to be familiar with the Scriptures. We must measure our thoughts, actions, and attitudes by the Word of God. Not our will, but His will be done (Luke 22:42).

## CHAPTER 13

# BELIEVING GOD'S WORD

*"For whatsoever things were written afore-time were written for our learning, that we through patience and comfort of the scriptures might have hope."*

**Romans 15:4**

God has given us wisdom in the Scriptures regarding how to raise our kids in His ways. His inspired Word, by the empowering of His spirit, will impart the patience we need and the reassurance of the authority God has given to us. Therefore, we can have great expectation of what He has in store for us personally and for our children.

As we have learned, the Biblical principles concerning discipline develops mutual respect between parent and child and increases our reverence and admiration for our loving God and His Holy Word. The acronym RESPECT simply helps us to retain the seven steps to correcting our child in love: Remember, Establish, Speak, Pray, Encourage, Correct, and Train. We have read the list and noted the suggestions. Now we come to the most important key concept of the Biblical precedence when it comes to how to discipline our child firmly and lovingly. We must learn to administer the necessary discipline without being abusive.

> *"For the wrath of man worketh not the righteousness of God."*
>
> *James 1:20*

**R**emember, we are to never respond in anger. We must learn to control our temper. No amount of ranting or raving will bring about desirable qualities in our child. We must be patient and wait for our emotions to calm down.

> *"...knowing that tribulation worketh patience; And patience, experience; and experience, hope..."*
>
> *Romans 5:3-4*

A child's willful disobedience in and of itself is an incredible ordeal that tries our patience. We may not be successful at first, but we must realize that it is the testing of our faith that is working persistence and fortitude into our lives. These experiences are constantly giving us the understanding of the certainty of God's Word, which gives us hope: the absolute expectation of coming good.

*"God is love."*

*1 John 4:8*

Establish the fact that God is love. This is a great first Scripture verse for all kids to memorize and learn at a very young age. They need to know that God loves them and cares about them individually. Since God is love, a close relationship with Him will produce the fruit of love in our lives. Love is natural to the character and nature of God. As we are more personally acquainted with God, we are more able, by the power of His Spirit, to walk in His light and love one another.

*"...God chastens those He loves."*

*Hebrews 12:6*

Because God loves us, He will lovingly correct us. All of us as God's children are under the influence of His loving discipline. Those of us who experience God's correction are being equipped by this learning process to train our children in righteousness and peace. As we submit to the correction of our Heavenly Father, it will be an example and an encouragement to our children to willfully comply.

*"...speaking the truth in love..."*
                              *Ephesians 4:15*

Speak in a normal conversational tone. It's really not helpful to raise our voices. Share and exemplify what the Bible has to say about loving correction. As parents, we should maintain truth in love, not only in our speech but also in our lifestyle.

*"Pleasant words are as an honeycomb, sweet to the soul, and health to the bones."*
                              *Proverbs 16:24*

Kind, supportive, caring, words spoken to our children encourage Godly instruction and make learning desirable; whereas, bitter, harsh, cruel or insensitive words produce just the opposite effect. Positive appropriately spoken words that encourage, soothe, and praise our children can be pleasurable and inspirational in helping them feel better physically, mentally, emotionally, and spiritually.

This Proverb reminds me of a story about a young boy who had been naughty and disobedient. During family devotions the father prayed for his son and mentioned a number of bad things the boy had done. Soon afterward the mother heard her five-year-old boy sobbing profusely. When she asked what was wrong, the boy cried out, "Daddy always tells God the bad things about me. He never tells Him the good things I do!"

This little boy's experience underscores a weakness that is much too common. Instead of recognizing the good in our children, we tend to notice their faults. Rather than speaking words that are edifying and uplifting, we are inclined to communicate negative or unpleasant feelings. Again, that's why it's important that we look at life through the lens of Scripture. We need to measure our thoughts, actions, attitudes, and speech by the Word of God. The concept of speaking gracious, appropriate, and pleasant words will be discussed in greater detail in the companion volume, *Directing Your Child In God's Ways.*

*"And, ye fathers, provoke not your children to wrath: but bring them up in the nurture and admonition of the Lord."*

*Ephesians 6:4*

As parents we are not to frustrate our children or incite them to anger by our insensitivity: saying things that we shouldn't, placing unreasonable demands upon them, or showing favoritism to their brother or sister. Such actions will only cause children to become discouraged and embittered. Instead, because we love our children, we raise them, care for them, encourage them, caution them, and correct them; thereby we are providing for their physical, emotional, and spiritual needs.

*"Children, obey your parents in the Lord: for this is right. Honour thy father and mother; which is the first commandment with promise; That it may be well with thee, and thou mayest live long on the earth."*

*Ephesians 6:1-3*

Share and explain what God's Word says about loving correction. Talk with our kids about what they did wrong, why they are in trouble, and what can be done to prevent this from happening again. Physically open the Bible, show them the Scriptures and read the verses aloud to them. Our children learn to obey "in the Lord" and we, as parents, learn to train and instruct "in the Lord." Jesus Christ desires to not only be the center of our interaction within our relationships but also the focus of our training and learning.

*"Pray without ceasing."*

*1 Thessalonians 5:17*

Pray without ceasing. Right! How does that work when we're in the midst of trying to discipline our child? Constant prayer isn't without interruptions, but our intention is to continue on, as we are able. Interruptions can be like a hacking cough—interrupting while we are trying to speak. We still persist in making our point in the midst of the interruptions. As parents we need to purpose to maintain continuous fellowship with the Lord as much as possible as we are disciplining our children in order that we might truly correct them in love.

**"Praying always with all prayer and supplication in the Spirit..."**

**Ephesians 6:18**

Continual prayer is so much easier when we are walking in the Spirit rather than carrying out the desires of our flesh. When we choose to pray—we are immediately empowered by the Spirit—our human tendency is not to pray.

**"If any of you lack wisdom, let him ask of God, that giveth to all men liberally, and upbraideth not; and it shall be given him."**

**James 1:5**

From the moment that our child has willfully disobeyed and needs correction, we must continually ask for God's guidance and direction. His help and support is willingly and generously accessible if we only ask.

*"But exhort one another daily, while it is called today; lest any of you be hardened through the deceitfulness of sin."*

*Hebrews 3:13*

Encourage one another each and every day. Support each other on a daily basis in loving obedience to God's Word. We should be very cautious to not allow our hearts to be hardened through unbelief. God's Word is true! Believe it, receive it, and act upon it!

*"Chasten thy son while there is hope, and let not thy soul spare for his crying."*

*Proverbs 19:18*

Correct your child while there is hope. This verse is very crucial. This command to discipline our child is a powerful word of warning against being unreceptive, passive parents. When our children are willfully disobedient, they should be corrected in their younger years while there is still hope for them. If we neglect the needed correction in their lives, it could ultimately lead to punishment under the laws of the land or to the natural consequences that are associated with inappropriate behavior. So, dear parent, we need to spank them, hug them, talk with them, pray with them, encourage them, and love on them. We do this in obedience to our loving Heavenly Father.

> *"Correct thy son, and he shall give thee rest; yea, he shall give delight unto thy soul."*
>
> *Proverbs 29:17*

Loving correction brings hope and peace. If we, as parents, will deal with the hassle of correcting our children now, the outcome will be joy and peace later. Our child will not only learn appropriate behavior but also will grow and mature through the discipline process.

> *"Train up a child in the way he should go: and when he is old, he will not depart from it."*
>
> *Proverbs 22:6*

Train up our child in God's ways. We are to dedicate them to the Lord. Lovingly training our children involves restricting their behavior away from the things that are destructive and directing them toward goodness and righteousness.

*"Be careful for nothing; but in every thing by prayer and supplication with thanksgiving let your requests be made known unto God. And the peace of God, which passeth all understanding, shall keep your hearts and minds through Christ Jesus."*

*Philippians 4:6-7*

We are encouraged not to be anxious or uptight about anything but with thanksgiving bring our prayers and petitions unto the Lord. Please notice that we bring our request to the Lord with thanksgiving—thanking Him in advance for what He is going to do and for what He has done.

These seven steps, if prayerfully applied, will bring a peace not only to our own hearts and lives but also to the lives of our children and family. This peace far surpasses our own understanding and will keep our hearts and minds focused upon Christ Jesus. His Word is true! May we believe it, receive it, and continue to act upon it! In Jesus' Name!

# APPENDIX A

# PARENT'S PRAYER

*L*ord help us to train up our children in Your ways so that when they are older they will not depart from You. Please give us understanding of Your Word and sensitivity to Your Holy Spirit that we will discipline our kids in a manner that would mold and shape their character into Your image. Strengthen and empower us to consistently use the rod of correction in a way that breaks the will of our children without breaking their spirit. May our discipline always be administered in love—not in anger or frustration. May our children learn to respect the rod of authority in their lives and in turn honor us, as their parents, and reverence You as their Lord and Savior. In faith, may we choose to receive and express forgiveness towards one another—bringing a peace *to our lives personally and to those around us. Above all, may we love You, Lord Jesus, with all of our heart, soul, mind, and strength and love one another as our self. We desire to learn from Your Word, from lessons in life, and from the experiences of others so that we do not have to unnecessarily endure difficulties and hardships. Lord help us to consistently place our faith in You and encourage one another in the things that we know to be right and true according to Your Word. May we continually be receptive to receiving the full counsel of Your Word and live our lives in a manner that would be honoring and pleasing in Your sight. We thank You for hearing our prayer and working these principles in and through our lives.*

*May You be exalted, lifted up and glorified!*

*In Jesus name we pray,*

*Amen*

## APPENDIX B

# PARENT'S CHECKLIST

## Seven Steps to Correcting Your Child in Love

**RESPECT – R**emember, **E**stablish, **S**peak, **P**ray, **E**ncourage, **C**orrect, **T**rain

1. **R**emember to never lash out in anger! (James 1:20). Our anger does not bring about God's righteousness.
2. **E**stablish that God is love (1 John 4:8), and that God corrects those He loves (Hebrews 12:6). Because we love our children we discipline them (Ephesians 6:4).
3. **S**peak in a normal conversational tone. Speak the truth in love (Ephesians 4:15). Share what the

Bible has to say about loving correction (Ephesians 6:1-2).

4. **P**ray without ceasing (1 Thessalonians 5:17). Praying always (Ephesians 6:18). From the moment correction is needed, continually ask for God's guidance and direction (James 1:5).

5. **E**ncourage one another (Hebrews 3:13). Support each other in loving obedience to God's Word.

6. **C**orrect your child while there is hope (Proverbs 19:18; 29:17). Loving correction brings hope and peace (Romans 15:4).

7. **T**rain up your child in God's ways (Proverbs 22:6).

These seven steps will not only develop mutual respect between parent and child but also increase our reverence and admiration for our loving Heavenly Father and His inspired Word.

Please review Chapters 10 and 13 for practical suggestions and applications of how to implement appropriate loving discipline.

Correcting and directing go hand in hand. We need to correct our children in love, but we must also direct them in His ways; therefore, a companion volume is presently underway, *Directing Your Child In God's Ways*.

## APPENDIX C

# WORKS CITED

Strong, James, *Hebrew And Chaldee Dictionary Accompanying The Exhaustive Concordance of The Bible*, 1890, Abingdon.

Merriam - Webster, *Webster's New Collegiate Dictionary*. 1976 ed. G & C Merriam Co.

*Family News In Focus*, "American College of Pediatricians Supports Spanking", December 11, 2007, <http://www.citizenlink.org/CL News/A000006098.cfm>

Trumbull, Den A., "Discipline of the Child," *Corporal Punishment: A Scientific Review of its Use in Discipline*. 2007, The American College of

Pediatricians,  <http://www.acpeds.org/?CO
NTEXT=art&cat=10005&art=166&BISKIT
=791621339>

Breinigsville, PA USA
15 October 2009
225930BV00002B/2/P